THE BOOK OF DAYS

THE BOOK OF DAYS

PERPETUAL CALENDAR

Featuring full-color images
from *The Papyrus of Ani* and zodiac
signs from the Temple of Isis at Denderah

INTRINSIC BOOKS
NEW YORK • MIAMI • CHICAGO

First published in 2014 by Intrinsic Books
www.intrinsicbooks.com

Distributed to the trade by
Red Wheel/Weiser, LLC
65 Parker St. • Suite 7
Newburyport, MA 01950
www.redwheelweiser.com

ISBN: 978-0-9718870-8-4

Library of Congress Cataloging-in-Publication Data
Available upon request

Intrinsic Books is the Book Packaging Partnership
between Specialty Book Marketing, Inc. and Studio 31, Inc.

The Book of Going Forth by Day:
The Complete Papyrus of Ani Featuring
Integrated Text and Full-Color Images
is published by Chronicle Books

The Denderah Zodiac
is published as a poster by Studio 31

Book design by Studio 31
www.studio31.com

Printed in China

This copy of
THE BOOK OF DAYS
belongs to

_____

A WORD ON
THE BOOK OF DAYS

The ancient Egyptians were extremely conscious of the ebb and flow of time. The annual inundation of the Nile was a key to their agricultural efforts, national survival, and cultural identity. Their calendar is one of humanity's oldest systems to mark the passage of time, dating back at least 6,000 years.

We have created *The Book of Days* to help commemorate significant occasions in our lives. The pace of the modern world makes a calendar such as this both a convenient reminder and a permanent record of those important events that form our character and memories—individual milestones and those experiences shared with family and friends, whose meaning illuminates our own lives and will be treasured by generations to come.

The timeless and beautiful illustrations that make up this book come from *The Book of Going Forth by Day: The Egyptian Book of the Dead*. These images continue to resonate some 3,500 years after being painted for the personal papyrus of the scribe Ani, in about 1250 BC during the Nineteenth Dynasty. Purchased in 1888 by E. A. Wallis Budge for the British Museum, *The Papyrus of Ani* is the longest, best preserved, most complete, and beautiful scroll yet discovered. We have included 60 of the 74 images of the papyrus in the same sequence as Ani's original.

Ani believed that this collection of spells would allow him and his wife Tutu to travel through the Underworld after their deaths and would free their souls to soar unencumbered in the celestial realms. These prayers, hymns, and spells derive from the much earlier *Pyramid Texts*, originally carved into the stone walls of the royal burial chambers of the Pharaohs beginning as early as 2400 BC. Later still, circa 2000 BC, prayers for the Afterlife became more widespread and nobles had them painted on their coffins—they thus became known as the *Coffin Texts*. Around 1550 BC, the hymns and spells began to be painted on rolls of papyrus—the *Books of the Dead*—an even more universal distribution that reached the middle class.

By 1886, Egyptologists began to standardize the numbering system for the chapters of the *Book of the Dead*. However, individual papyri were arranged at the discretion of their owners and creators, thus defying standardization. This explains the nonsequential numbering of chapters you will find in the following pages.

The Egyptian Book of the Dead may seem obscure; it does not follow Western logical forms. Ancient Egyptian religion was never a unity, nor did it maintain either an established orthodoxy or a textual canon. We hope the list of Egyptian gods and goddesses at the back of this book may help make the characters of the scroll somewhat more accessible.

The astrological images reproduced here come from the ancient Egyptian zodiac found on the ceiling of the Temple of Isis at Denderah. While the zodiac appears to have been carved around 100 BC, it has been linked to earlier astronomical drawings. Egyptologists have suggested that it represents midnight of the Summer Solstice of 700 BC, when Sirius rose at dawn with the Sun—long anticipated by ancient astronomers. The Hellenistic style of the twelve zodiacal figures shows the influence of the Ptolemaic Dynasty that ruled Egypt from 305 to 35 BC. Napoleon's troops removed the zodiac in 1799 and it now hangs in the Louvre. (Please note that the date ranges given for each astrological sign vary slightly from year to year.)

If you would like further information on *The Papyrus of Ani* please see the Wasserman/Goelet edition of *The Egyptian Book of the Dead: The Book of Going Forth by Day*. There you will find a full reproduction of the papyrus with a complete translation of the hieroglyphics, a glossary of terms and concepts, as well as an introduction and extensive commentary. We thank Dr. Goelet for his commentary, which has been freely adopted for many of the plate captions shown here.

We hope you will enjoy your copy of *The Book of Years*. Ani and Tutu's papyrus records their most intimate and personal journey through the trials of the Egyptian Afterlife. May their success serve as an inspiration and metaphor for our lives today.

www.JamesWassermanBooks.com
www.EgyptianBookOfDead.com
EgyptianBookDead.com

In the opening vignette of the papyrus, Ani and his wife Tutu stand before two tables of offerings as they prepare to begin the mysterious journey through the Afterlife. The visible damage to the nearly perfectly preserved scroll is due to this section being at the outermost part of the roll. The *menat* and *sistrum* in Tutu's hands were musical instruments used to accompany ritual singing and recitation. *The Book of Going Forth by Day* was meant to assist Tutu on her journey as well as Ani. The text is a hymn to the Sun God Ra as He rises in the east.

JANUARY

	1
	2
	3
	4
	5
	6
	7

JANUARY

8

9

10

11

12

13

14

Isis (left) and Nephthys (right), the two sisters, twin aspects of the God-dess represent Her celestial (Isis) and terrestrial (Nephthys) natures. They kneel in adoration before a tripartite image. It includes the *ankh,* the Egyptian symbol of life and regeneration, which stands upon a *djed* pillar, signifying the human spine, and stability. The red solar disk on top is held by the hands of the *ankh.* The conjoining of these three symbols may signify Osiris-Ra, the celestial and the underworld aspects of the male God, balancing perfectly with His dual female counterparts.

Ani and Tutu are shown again before two offering stands as they assume postures of prayer and worship. On Tutu's head is a cone of scented fat, decorated with an open flower. This type of headdress was worn by both men and women for banquets and other indoor ceremonial affairs where perfume was desirable. Egyptian women sang and played music during religious ceremonies. Here Tutu is accompanying Ani as he recites the beautiful hymn to Osiris that comprises the text of this plate.

15

16

17

18

19

20

21

The critical moment of the papyrus is the Weighing of the Heart, or the Judgment of the Dead. Ani and Tutu enter a hall. Here Ani's heart is shown on the Balances, weighed against the Feather of Truth of Maat, Lady of Justice. The heart symbolizes the sum total of Ani's life and deeds while on earth. If it balances against the feather, he will be allowed to proceed. If not, Ani will be devoured by Ammit, the composite monster on the far right. Anubis, Lord of Embalming, tends the scales, as the ibis-headed Thoth, God of Wisdom and of Writing, records the results. The

entire proceeding is observed by the Great Tribunal above. The text begins with Ani's prayer that his heart will not speak against him as he stands before the assembly who will pass judgement upon him. The text continues as Thoth and the Tribunal proclaim that Ani's heart has been found pure. This is one of the earliest examples in religious iconography and literature of a person's purity of life on earth, and the condition of his soul, being judged by a higher authority for admission to a state of grace after death. It is a theme developed by many later religions.

JANUARY

22

23

24

25

26

27

28

JANUARY

29

30

31

AQUARIUS
JANUARY 20–FEBRUARY 19

Now that Ani has successfully passed through the ordeal of the Weighing Scene, he is led by the falcon-headed Horus, son of Isis and Osiris, into the presence of Osiris, Lord of the Underworld and God of Resurrection. Horus announces that Ani has been judged and his heart found pure. Ani offers a prayer of praise and supplication to Osiris. He states that he has been "vindicated" before the God. However, although his soul has been found pure, Ani is not out of danger. Horus asks that Ani be given bread and beer to fortify him for his upcoming journey through the Underworld and the dangerous forces he will there encounter.

FEBRUARY

1

2

3

4

5

6

7

FEBRUARY

8

9

10

11

12

13

14

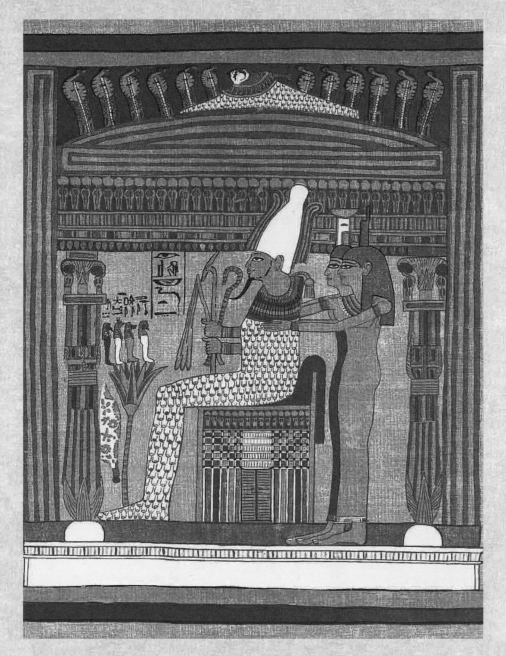

Osiris is shown seated while holding His three characteristic symbols of authority: the *was* scepter; the shepherd's crook; and the flail or whip. At the top of the kiosk the hawk-headed Sokar illustrates the nighttime journey of the Sun. In front of Osiris stand the Four Sons of Horus, while behind Him are His wife and sister Isis, beside Her sister Nepthys. Osiris, a principal figure in the Papyrus of Ani, is one of the earliest resurrection gods—an earthly king martyred by the forces of evil, He lives again as a promise to humanity of life after bodily death. Osiris's green face indicates the vernal renewal and rebirth in the Afterlife.

The papyrus continues, "Here begin the chapters of going out into the day, the praises and recitations for going to and fro in the God's Domain." The subject matter of this and the next three vignettes is the funeral. The four servants at the top left are carrying various items to be placed in Ani's tomb. Below, mourners attend a large chest upon which rests the god Anubis. The chest holds the internal organs of Ani, which are preserved in four canopic jars. Shown at right are the chief male mourners who follow the casket in which rests Ani's mummy.

FEBRUARY

15

16

17

18

19

20

21

The procession continues with Ani's bier resting on a ceremonial boat, imitating the great celestial bark in which the gods travel through the heavens. Tutu kneels in grief beside her husband. Tiny mummified figures of Isis and Nephthys, in front of and behind Ani's mummy, further identify him with Osiris and His renewal in death. A priest, whose white robe is covered with a panther skin, turns to offer incense in a libation. Four men guide the tow-rope at right. The full plate (not shown here) illustrates four oxen dragging the tow-rope ahead of the men.

FEBRUARY

22

23

24

25

26

27

28

29

PISCES
FEBRUARY 20–MARCH 20

As the funeral march forges ahead, we see two of the three men who are carrying various grave goods that they will place before the tomb (shown in the next plate). The female mourners are grouped together facing both in the direction of the advancing procession and in the direction of the tomb scene ahead. Their bared breasts were a characteristic Egyptian sign of mourning and bereavement. In contrast to the emotionally controlled stoic faces of the male mourners (shown earlier), the cheeks of these female mourners are streaked with tears.

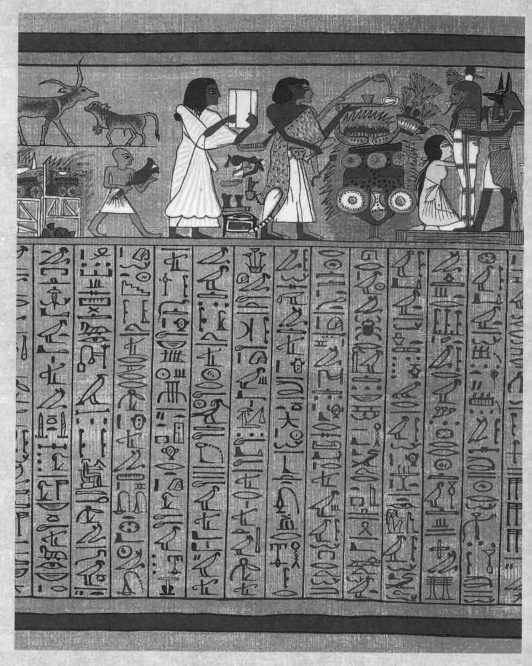

The procession arrives at Ani's tomb. At left, in a poignant scene, the freshly severed leg of a calf is carried by an officiating priest for use in the Opening-of-the-Mouth ceremony taking place at right. One priest is reciting various prayers, while the other two in panther skins are conducting the ceremony. Various consecrated objects equip Ani with the power to face the trials of the Afterlife that loom ahead. Tutu kneels to pay her last respects to her husband. Anubis is shown grasping Ani's mummy which He will carry to its final resting place within the tomb.

MARCH

1

2

3

4

5

6

7

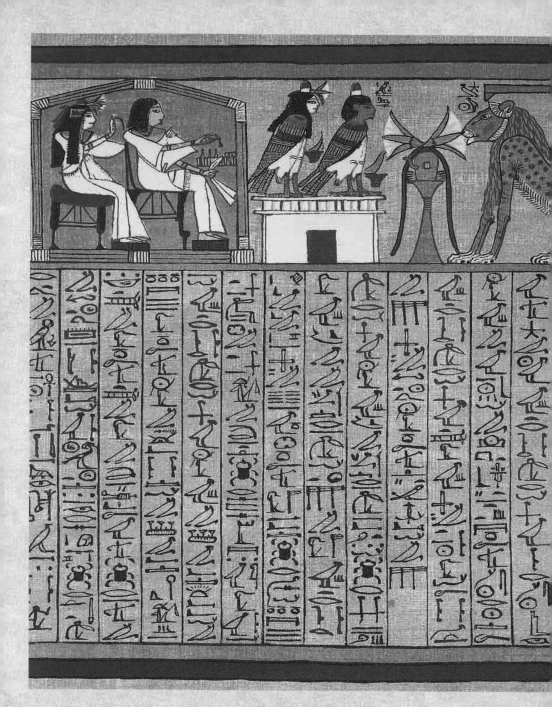

This next group of eight plates composes Spell 17, an introduction to the Afterlife, the "going in and out of God's Domain." Ani and Tutu are shown in a tent where Ani plays *senet* without an opponent. In this context, the game is an allegory for the transition to a successful Afterlife. Next, we see the couple as two *ba*-birds. The personification of the purpose of the Papyrus of Ani, the *ba*-bird symbolizes the freedom of the human soul to travel at will through the Empyrean.

MARCH

8

9

10

11

12

13

14

MARCH

15

16

17

18

19

20

21

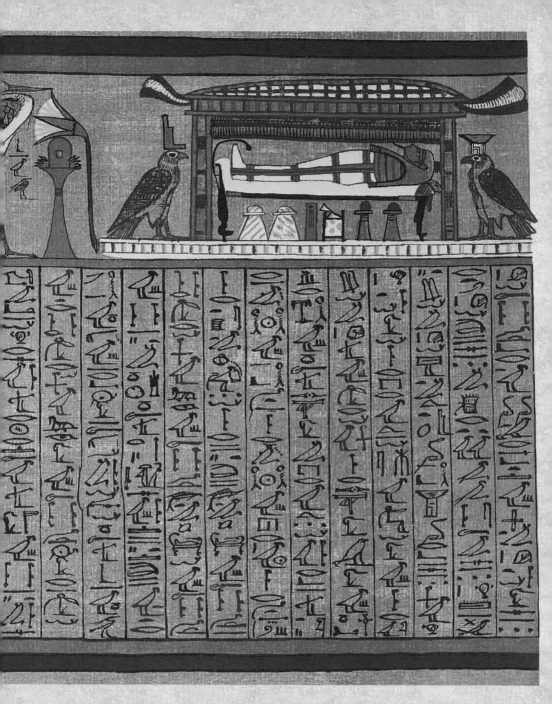

Other images follow (not included here), until we come to Ani's mummiform coffin, lying on a lion bed in a shrine. To the left and right of the coffin are the "Two Kites," representative of the goddesses Isis (left) and Nephthys (right). Their bird forms are those of the common raptor, whose cries were interpreted by the Egyptians as sounds of mourning. The pennants shown streaming from either side of the coffin may symbolize the "breath of life."

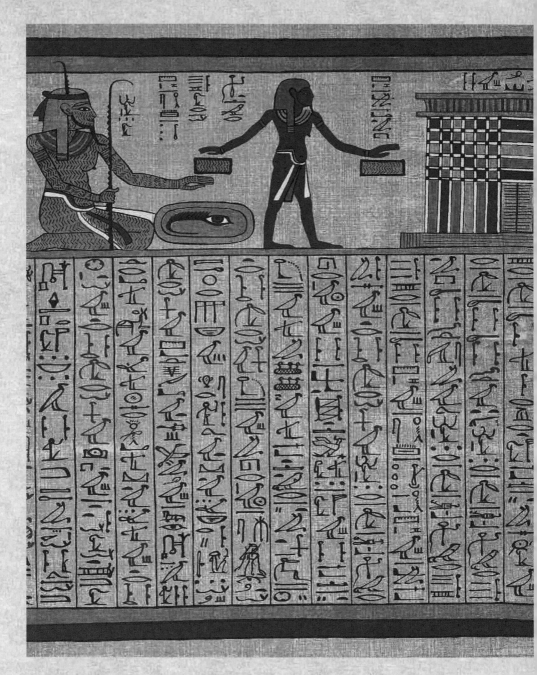

At left is Heh, "Millions of Years," and Wadj-wer, "Sea," both shown as androgynous beings with beards and breasts. Heh's blue color and rippled aspect identify him with water. This is one of the few uses of the color blue in the papyrus. The paint was made with crushed lapis-lazuli. Heh's left hand extends over an oval containing a reduced image of the famous *wadjet*-eye, seen throughout Egyptian art (as well as on the Great Seal of the United States). The open eye of God, surveying all within its kingdom, is an appropriate symbol of the omnipresence of the Divine.

MARCH

22

23

24

25

26

27

28

Chapter 17 continues as Ani rises from the Mound of Abydos. Two hands emerge from the chest, each holding an *ankh*. On either side of Ani are the Four Sons of Horus: these are the ape-headed Hapy; the human-headed Imsety; the jackal-headed Duamutef; and the falcon-headed Qebehsenuef. The Four Sons are called the Lords of Justice of the Tribunal "who put terror into the doers of wrong." Depicted as well on the chest in front of Ani, their forms are traditionally carved on the four canopic jars in which the internal organs of the deceased are preserved.

29

30

31

ARIES
MARCH 21–APRIL 19

APRIL

1

2

3

4

5

6

7

The figures here and on the next plate are part of a group of eleven deities seated on a reed mat. They are named in the hieroglyphics above their heads. They are also identified in the text as "behind the Great Bear in the northern sky." Chapter 17 represents one of several initiation rituals that form *The Book of Going Forth by Day*. There is a dialog between the soul of the candidate and the gods and archetypes of the Afterlife. This long chapter serves as both an instruction and as a test. The series of questions must be properly answered for the soul to continue its journey.

8

9

10

11

12

13

14

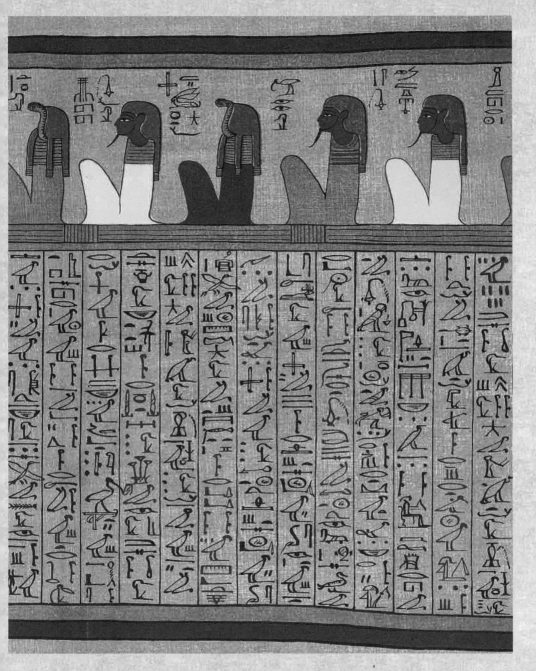

The group of deities continues from the previous plate. Ani and Tutu will pass by each of these guardians, who will both protect and cleanse them of any evils accumulated since birth. They will further ascertain the couple's moral and magical fitness to proceed. Ani and Tutu will strive to join the "guild" of the divine by learning the keys to the various riddles and questions posed to them throughout this long spell. The text serves as a theological overview of the Afterlife. It was part of the curriculum an Egyptian was expected to study during his or her life.

The two *djed*-pillars frame a shrine on which Ra is shown in falcon form. The human-headed bird wearing the White Crown of Upper Egypt is probably Osiris. Ra, the Stellar God, and Osiris, God of the Underworld, are the primary deities of the Egyptian Afterlife. The Great Cat, a manifestation of the Sun God, slays a snake, a representation of Apophis, the Enemy. At right Tutu is kneeling before the prow of the Sun-Bark.

APRIL

15

16

17

18

19

20

21

APRIL

22

23

24

25

26

27

28

Chapter 17 continues. It is the longest and one of the oldest chapters of *The Book of Going Forth by Day*. Here, the god Atum, Lord of the Evening Sun, is seated within a solar disk. At his right, resting upon a shrine-like plinth, is the Lion God Rehu. Above Him, a uraeus serpent is entwined around a bouquet of lotus flowers. In front, an open lotus blossom rests on an offering stand. This is the final scene of Spell 17.

Ani and Tutu stand before a group of deities in a vertically split panel comprised of two separate chapters (147 above and 146 below). They approach a series of seven Gates above, each guarded by three seated figures—a gatekeeper, a guardian, and an announcer. The lower register introduces a series of ten Portals, each guarded by one gatekeeper. The candidate, the deceased, must be in possession of secret knowledge.

29

30

TAURUS
APRIL 20–MAY 20

MAY

1

2

3

4

5

6

7

The figures in chapters 147 and 146 have names that Ani must know, and demand speeches that he must properly deliver. Such esoteric knowledge would be mastered during one's lifetime. If the candidate succeeds in this demonstration of spiritual fitness, he will pass unmolested, and "He shall be yonder as a lord of eternity, in one flesh with Osiris."

The couple prepares to enter before a series of Divine Councils who will demand further precise ritual behavior. An important function of the priests robed in the panther skins was the ceremony of the Opening-of-the-Mouth. Here the priests introduce Ani and Tutu to the deities ahead.

MAY

8

9

10

11

12

13

14

15

16

17

18

19

20

21

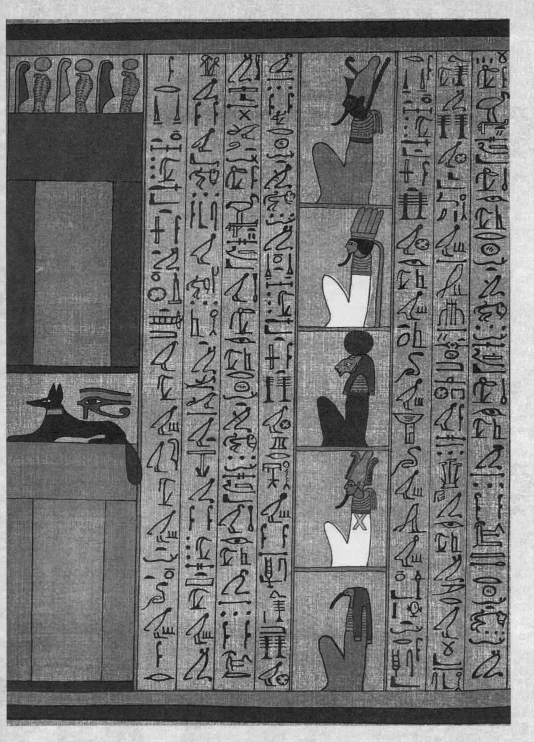

The text above begins with an invocation of Thoth and a prayer for His protection. Like Chapter 17, this is a formalized initiation. The guardians must be satisfied with the answers provided by Ani so that the couple may be admitted and allowed to continue on their journey.

MAY

22

23

24

25

26

27

28

The deities in Chapter 18 are among the most powerful and important of the Egyptian pantheon. In the previous plate we see (top to bottom) Atum, Shu, Tefnut, Osiris, and Thoth. In this plate, at left are Osiris, Horus, two *wadjet*-eyes above two shrines, and Thoth. In the second column are Horus, Isis, and two of the sons of Horus: Imsety, and Hapy.

29

30

31

GEMINI
MAY 21–JUNE 20

Each column composes a "council" of the deities portrayed. The chapter ends with a rubric—a commentary written in red ink—declaring that if one recites the spell while pure, it means going forth by day after burial. Furthermore, this incantation brings prosperity on earth with the ability to emerge from every fire and be free from every evil.

At left, we see the all important ceremony of the Opening-of-the-Mouth. The ritual is conducted by a *sem*-priest covered with a panther skin. Ani is depicted as a statue seated upon a *maat*-sign base. The priest strikes Ani's likeness with the snake-shaped adze—a chisel designed to pry open the mouth of the deceased. This will free Ani to speak as in life— to be able to make his case before the Great Gods, to utter the magic spells by which he may achieve power and protection in the Afterlife.

JUNE

1

2

3

4

5

6

7

JUNE

8

9

10

11

12

13

14

Ani is holding a small billowing sail that represents his breath being restored in the God's Domain. He is next shown with a handkerchief and walking stick. Ani proceeds on to the next vignette where he adores a heart on an offering table. He is praying before four seated deities that his heart may be protected. The role of the heart is critical in Egypt— it represents the mind as well as the moral essence of the individual.

On the left, Ani and Tutu wade in a tree-lined pool. While refreshing themselves with water in the coolness of the shade, they undergo another initiation ritual in which Ani must answer certain questions. In the next vignette a tree goddess pours water into his hands. At right, Ani is seated before a table holding victuals that will sustain him. The walking stick in his left hand indicates this is merely a rest stop on his journey.

JUNE

15

16

17

18

19

20

21

Ani is standing in the west facing east—the only time in the entire papyrus he does so. While he is shown in a posture of adoration before three gods, each holding *was*-scepters and *ankhs*, the text makes clear that Ani is actually threatening them with the fury of his displeasure if he is ill-treated. At right, he holds his scribal palette, while a ferryman holds a flail. Ani insists that his direction of travel is the Blessed West. He identifies himself with Osiris and demands to be protected and obeyed.

JUNE

22

23

24

25

26

27

28

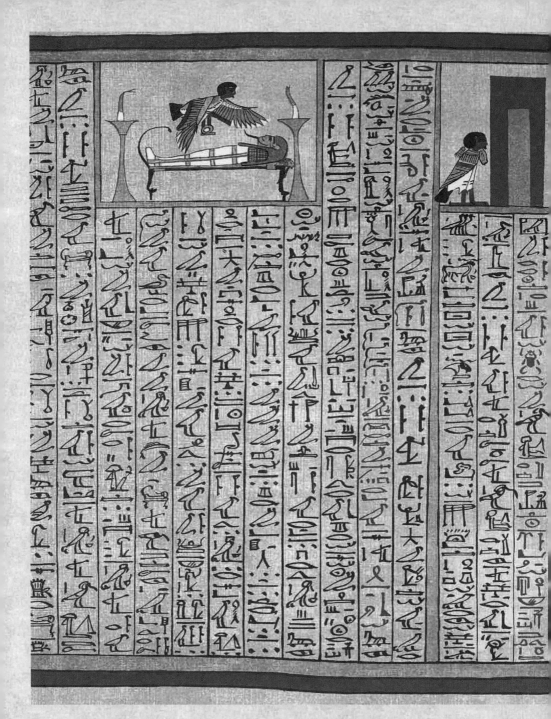

Above is the all-important Spell 89, designed to allow the *ba* of Ani to rejoin his corpse in the God's Domain. Ani's *ba* is shown holding the *shen* symbol of cyclical eternity and protection. The reuniting of the *ba* with the body represents the critical moment of awakening the power to go forth in the Afterlife. The vignette at right shows Ani's *ba* before the doorway to Eternity, free to travel without hindrance.

29

30

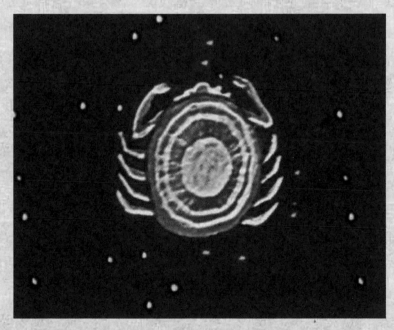

CANCER
JUNE 21–JULY 22

The vignettes above and accompanying texts address the freedom to travel "swift-footed when going out from the earth." At left, the symbolic boat (the *henu*-bark) of the god Sokar was carried on the shoulders of priests during processions. In the center, the falcon on the round-topped standard with a feather is a representation of the hieroglyph for the West. At right, the ram whom Ani adores is another symbol for the *ba*.

JULY

1

2

3

4

5

6

7

Ani is standing before a doorway, which may indicate that he is able to see his house on earth. Next, he treads upon a snake while spearing it. The snake in Egypt, as elsewhere, represents the negative force, or enemies, over whom Ani triumphs. At right is a beautiful hymn to Ra as He travels in His bark at the uprising of the Sun—the Dawn Prayer of praise.

JULY

8

9

10

11

12

13

14

This magnificient vignette balances the human worshippers with the divinities they adore as Ani and Tutu stand before Osiris and Isis. The identification of human and divine is characteristic of Egyptian religious beliefs. This text consists of an address and a hymn to Osiris. The hieroglyphs above Ani and Tutu give their names and titles—the only place in the papyrus where Tutu's titulary appears. Osiris is addressed both

as the King of the Dead, *and* as the living "King of Upper and Lower Egypt." The royal uraeus serpent on His crown further emphasizes earthly kingship, as does His beard, fastened with a chin strap. Isis, the primary female deity of Egypt, wife and sister of Osiris, also wears the royal uraeus on Her vulture headdress, symbolic of an earthly queen. The throne on the top of Her crown is Her characteristic symbol of divinity.

JULY

15

16

17

18

19

20

21

JULY

22

23

24

25

26

27

28

Earlier, we saw Ani performing the Morning Adoration. Here, he worships Ra while standing in the sacred bark itself. The white bird at left is a swallow, a migratory species associated with the Sun God. The swallow's annual reappearance after some months of absence made it a fitting symbol of regeneration. The bird is standing on a colorful decorated straw mat, often shown at the prow of the solar bark and in tomb scenes.

29

30

31

LEO
JULY 23–AUGUST 22

AUGUST

1

2

3

4

5

6

7

The series of solar hymns continues. Here we see Ra in His bark facing a star-studded stele, presumably the night sky. Ani is not present. The rubric of Chapter 133 explains that its words are to be recited over a statue of the solar bark carved of malachite. The sky and the stars are to be purified with natron and incense. The figure of Ra is to be painted with ochre. An image of the spirit you desire to accompany Ra shall be placed in the bark and will thus be empowered.

AUGUST

8	
9	
10	
11	
12	
13	
14	

Here is Chapter 134. The vignette shows Ra and a huge solar disk riding together in the sacred bark. Again, the beautiful solar hymn of praise to the deity is accompanied by magical instructions explaining that a model of the boat and the deity should be built. Then, the gods of the Sacred Ennead are to be painted on a new bowl and placed in the bark, along with an image of the spirit to accompany them.

Curiously, Ani's papyrus repeats Chapter 18 (previously presented in the month of May). In its second appearance, the design of the vignettes is totally different. Instead of the earlier columnar layout, the deities of the pantheon are displayed in a horizontal row at the top of the papyrus. Previously, Ani and Tutu were introduced to the asembly by two panther-skin-clad priests who perform the Opening-of-the-Mouth ceremony. Here, Ani and Tutu climb the ladder shown at left.

AUGUST

15

16

17

18

19

20

21

AUGUST

22

23

24

25

26

27

28

While the deities of Chapter 18 are the most important in Egypt, the order in which they appear the second time varies slightly from the earlier sequence. What is crucial, however, is the central theme—Ani praying that the deities of the various councils will "vindicate" him, freeing him from the bonds of human mortality and sin. Ani beseeches them to accept him as morally, ethically, and magically worthy to participate with them as a legitimate resident of the Afterlife.

In Chapter 124, Ani and Tutu address three seated deities, described as doorkeepers of Osiris "who pacified the Two Lands" (Upper and Lower Egypt). Ani is desperately concerned with the quality of his food in the Afterlife—he knows the Afterlife is filled with cthonic forces and dramatic reversals of the ordered conventions of life on earth. Ani declares that he will not be forced to consume disgusting substances and prays that he and Tutu will be nourished with the bounty of the worthy.

29

30

31

VIRGO
AUGUST 23–SEPTEMBER 22

Here is a spell to transform Ani into a divine falcon. The falcon is a solar deity, a free-flying warrior soaring through the heavens, attaining the very highest vantage point in all of nature. His swiftness and concentration, his amazingly precise eyesight, and the ruthless determination of his hunting prowess make the falcon a symbol of freedom, panoramic vision, and otherwordly power. The Egyptians sought the ability to rise from the strictures of death and soar unimpeded through the Afterlife.

SEPTEMBER

1

2

3

4

5

6

7

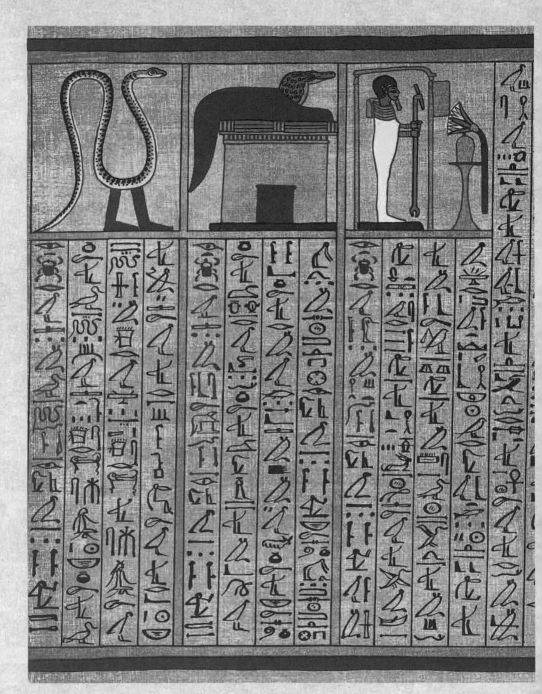

Above are three transformation spells. The snake symbolizes rejuvenation and rebirth, shedding its skin and thus renewing itself. The crocodile inspires fear. Stronger than his foes, he is "immersed in dread." Transforming into Ptah (at right) guarantees one will not be forced to eat filth, but instead feast on bread and become as a "Lord of the Earth." The successful participant in the Egyptian Afterlife experienced the highest pleasures of the living—from drinking beer to making love.

SEPTEMBER

8

9

10

11

12

13

14

15

16

17

18

19

20

21

The ram deity Atum, Father of All the Gods, stands on a tomb with a candle. Here Ani identifies himself with the soul of Ra, the Lord of Light. Ani declares that he detests death. His transformation into the Benu-bird follows. The heron was said to have appeared on the primordial mound when land first emerged from water and the Light was brought forth. The heron gives Ani the power to go forth into the day after his death, and to share in the food of Osiris and the strength of Ra.

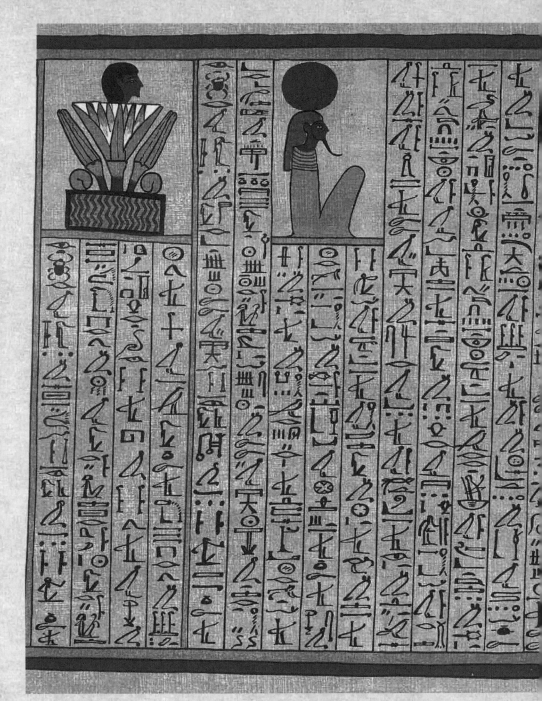

Ani's head rests on a lotus flower in a characteristic depiction of the god Nefertum, who shares a relationship with Ra as a creative deity. The next vignette of the seated Ra with the solar disk on his head illustrates a curious spell. Its title refers to transforming oneself into a god, and giving light and darkness. The text describes great magic and mythic power. It identifies the adept simultaneously with both male and female deities.

SEPTEMBER

22

23

24

25

26

27

28

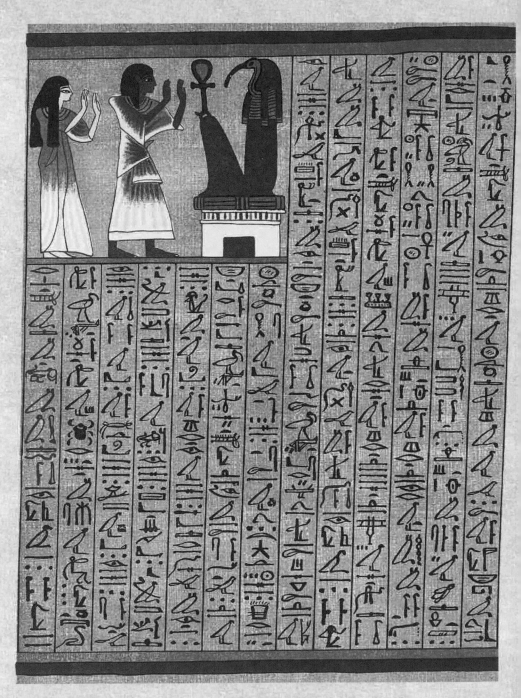

Ani and Tutu adore Thoth, the Lord of Wisdom and of Utterance. Thoth is seated upon a tomb balancing an *ankh* upon his knees. Ani complains of the evil unleashed in both this earthly world and the next. He describes a war between the forces of darkness and light. He seeks the power of life, of not dying again, of making love. In a dialog with Atum, Ani is happily assured that he shall live for millions of years—until the earth shall return to the primordial waters and Atum transform Himself again.

SEPTEMBER

29

30

LIBRA
SEPTEMBER 23–OCTOBER 22

This stunning tableau should be compared to that shown in mid-July.
There, the worshippers are similar in height to Osiris and Isis. Here the
human beings seem restored to the position of devotees or acolytes of the
powerful deities. The Four Sons of Horus stand upon the lotus in front
of Osiris. This chapter is considered an introduction to the crucial Chapter 125, the Negative Confession, that follows. The offering table is filled

with bounteous food and flowers. Ani and Tutu seek to learn the correct speech by which they may flourish in their upcoming visit to the Hall of the Two Truths where they will be judged. Ani has already been "vindicated"—his heart was weighed in the Balance and found worthy. Here he is questioned by Anubis. Ani must demonstrate the knowledge of the mysteries of the gods so that he may continue on.

OCTOBER

1

2

3

4

5

6

7

OCTOBER

8

9

10

11

12

13

14

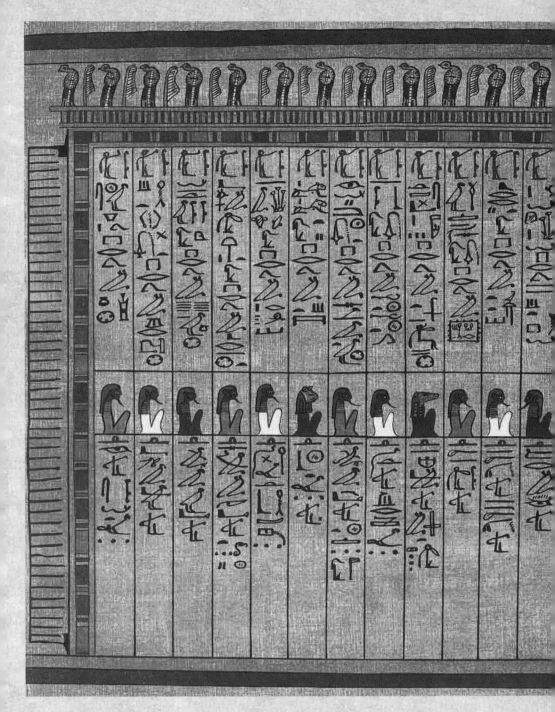

This beautifully framed image is one of the most important chapters of *The Book of the Dead*, conclusively demonstrating the influence of Egyptian theology on succeeding religions. Known as the "Negative Confession," it anticipates the Ten Commandments. The text here lists a series of forty-two sins which Ani proclaims he has not committed. Ani's "I have not" become the later "Thou shalt not." Among the virtues shared

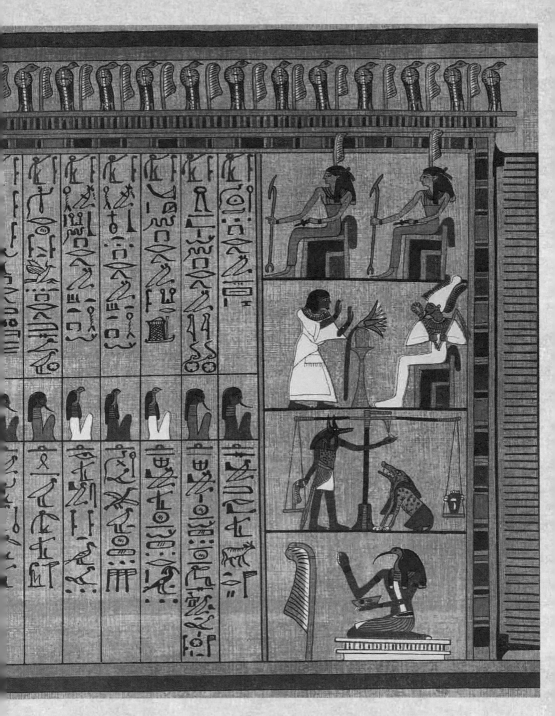

with the Ten Commandments are prohibitions against killing, stealing, lying, adultery, abjuring religious duties, and blasphemy. One ancient moral guidepost of the Egyptians that our society has lost sight of is: "I have brought no lawsuits." These highly moral people repeatedly expressed their ethical tenets with complete clarity throughout many of the chapters of *The Book of Going Forth by Day*.

OCTOBER

15

16

17

18

19

20

21

OCTOBER

22

23

24

25

26

27

28

29

30

31

SCORPIO
OCTOBER 23–NOVEMBER 21

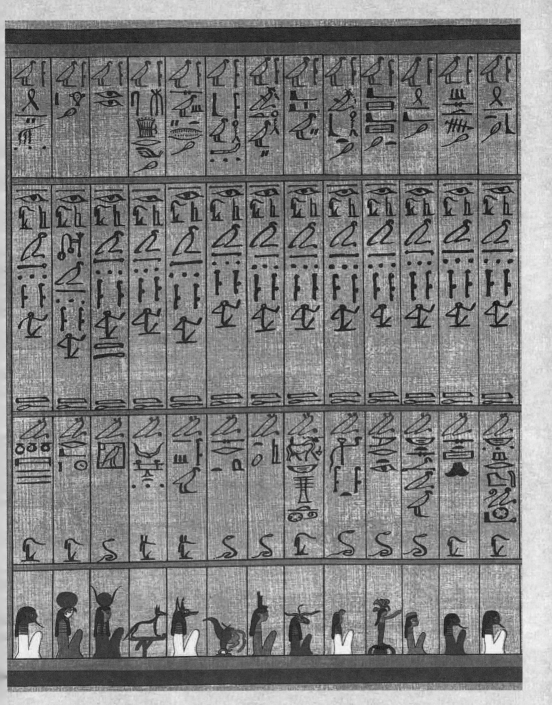

In Spell 42, Ani identifies each of the parts of his body with a deity. Thus he says, "My hair is Nun; my face is Ra; my eyes are Hathor...." Ani methodically continues all the way down to his toes and then states, "there is no member of mine devoid of a god, and Thoth is the protection of all my flesh." Having now made himself wholly divine, Ani is invulnerable to cthonic antagonists.

The dog-headed ape is a lower reflection of and companion to the ibis-headed Thoth. The four cynocephalic apes above are seated between flaming braziers around a lake of fire. At right is a *djed*-pillar amulet that will be placed on the throat of the deceased to make him a worthier spirit. The *tiyet* or Isis-knot amulet at right is placed on the neck. It brings the protection of Isis and the rejoicing of her son Horus.

NOVEMBER

1

2

3

4

5

6

7

The extraordinary vignette for Chapter 151 is a schematic representation of Ani's burial chamber. Totally balanced, it begins in the top register with the dual proclamation by Ani's *ba* at both ends. Following are the statements of two of Horus' sons Hapy (left) and Imsety (right). In the center is the stabilizing *djed*-pillar. The middle register shows the dual flames of protection that ward off enemies. Isis and Nephthys offer their

aid to Ani. In the center, Anubis prepares Ani's mummy in ceremonial fashion. Along the bottom, the *shabti* figures on the outside pledge their willingness to perform any physical labor demanded of "the Osiris Ani." Next Qebehsenuef and Duamutef, the other two sons of Horus, identitfy the spirit of Ani as that of their own father. In the center, Anubis rests atop a shrine, shown with a flagellum and wearing a protective collar.

NOVEMBER

8	
9	
10	
11	
12	
13	
14	

NOVEMBER

15

16

17

18

19

20

21

In Chapter 110, the couple is again offering bouquets. They have passed through the most dangerous parts of the Afterlife journey and are approaching the serenity of the "justified" or "vindicated." They stand before the paradise of the Field of Reeds at the entrance to the celestial realm. They will now be treated as included among the "blessed dead."

NOVEMBER

22

23

24

25

26

27

28

Ani stands in adoration before Ra, or Ra-Harakhty, with two open lotus flowers on offering stands. The entire vignette is drawn within a frame. Spell 148 is primarily concerned with guaranteeing consistent provisions for Ani's spirit in the God's Domain. Ani states that the seven celestial cows and their husband, the earthly bull below, will consistently pro-

vide him with bread and beer. In return for their generosity, he offers his allegiance. Ani similarly addresses the four Steering-oars, which may be thought of as guiding the celestial bark through the Heavens. Ra is called the "helmsman." At right are the fathers and the mothers of the gods who reign over sky and earth. Ani beseeches their protection.

29

30

SAGITTARIUS
NOVEMBER 22–DECEMBER 21

DECEMBER

1

2

3

4

5

6

7

Chapter 185 shows Ani and Tutu in adoration before a deity—identified in the hieroglyphics near His *Atef*-crown as "Sokar-Osiris, the Lord of the Secret Place, the Great God, Lord of the God's Domain." He is shown as hawk-headed, yet with most of the characteristic features of Osiris—

holding a shepherd's crook, flail, and *was*-scepter. This deity is wrapped in bandages and stands in the mummiform posture typical of Osiris. The falcon's head implies a celestial aspect to this syncretized deity, as if He incorporates rulership of both the Heavens and the Underworld.

DECEMBER

8

9

10

11

12

13

14

DECEMBER

15

16

17

18

19

20

21

DECEMBER

22

23

24

25

26

27

28

The goddess Tawaret stands upon a shrine-like plinth. She is a composite being whose body is that of a pregnant hippopotamus, with the fore legs and hind legs of a lioness, and a crocodile's tail. The largest table of offerings in the papyrus seems to celebrate Ani's success.

DECEMBER

29

30

31

CAPRICORN
DECEMBER 22–JANUARY 19

At last we come to Ani's resting place in the Blessed West, a simple pyramid-topped tomb with an open door. The horned goddess Hathor stands in a thicket of papyrus plants. Her eye is the *wadjet*-eye of Horus and Ra. The closing border frame clearly marks the end of the papyrus.

NOTES

NOTES

NOTES

NOTES

NOTES

NOTES

NOTES

NOTES

GODS OF THE BOOK OF DAYS

Ammit: Hybrid monster present at the Weighing of the Heart who consumes the souls of the unworthy.

Anubis: Jackal-headed god of embalming and the Underworld.

Apophis: A serpent deity, He is a force of Chaos, and arch-enemy of the Sun God.

Atum: Great primeval deity of Heliopolis, "the self-engendered one" who created the first gods, god of the setting sun.

Duamutef: Jackal-headed son of Horus, protector of the stomach of the deceased.

Hapy: Ape-headed son of Horus, protector of the lungs of the deceased.

Hathor: Cow-headed goddess of love, She is the patroness of the West, and a major figure in the Aterlife. Eventually, a deceased woman might be called, for example, "the Hathor Tutu."

Heh: "Millions of Years." A minor deity associated with water, called a Chaos god, and depicted as androgynous.

Horus: An important and early deity. He is the falcon-headed son of Isis and Osiris, the avenger of His father's murder, and thus the opponent of Seth.

Imsety: Human-headed son of Horus, protector of the liver of the deceased.

Isis: Celestial goddess, she is the Egyptian divine mother. She is the wife and sister of Osiris, sister of Nepthys and Seth, and the mother of Horus.

Maat: Lady of Truth, justice, balance, and the cosmic order. Her symbol is an ostrich feather.

Nefertum: God of the Lotus, son of Ptah and Sekmet, he is associated with Ra.

Nephys: Goddess of Nature, sister of Isis and Osiris, sister and consort of Seth, mother of Anubis.

Osiris: God of the Dead and the Underworld, husband and brother of Isis, He is the mythic king of Egypt who was murdered by His brother Seth. His name is affixed to the dead, i.e, "the Osiris Ani."

Ptah: One of the oldest deities, He is the Creator god of Memphis, the divine craftsman, and is depicted in human form.

Qebhsenuef: Falcon-headed son of Horus, protector of large intestine of deceased.

Ra (Re): Falcon-headed Sun god, arguably most important in Egyptian pantheon, the celestial counterpart of Osiris.

Ra-Harakty: Ra of the Two Horizons.

Rehu: A Lion god sometimes called, "the phallus of Ra."

Sekmet: Most important of the Lion goddesses, She is a symbol of destructive force, and sexual energy and passion. Protector of children and consort of Ptah.

Seth: Egyptian god of storms and the desert, an outsider, the negative force, murderer of Osiris and rival of Horus.

Shu: God of the Air, He is a member of the Heliopolitan Ennead and consort of the Lion goddess Tefnut.

Sokar: Falcon-headed god of the dead in the Memphite theology.

Sokar-Osiris: Falcon-headed, mummified, syncretic deity of the Afterlife.

Tawaret: "The Great One," a composite deity, Her main function is as a protector of women and children, especially in childbirth. Perhaps she is a fitting symbol of Ani's rebirth in the Afterlife.

Tefnut: Lion goddess, associated with moisture, She is the daughter of Atum and sister and wife of Shu.

Thoth: Divine scribe, He is the Lord of Wisdom, the word, measurement, communication, writing, and science.

Wadj-wer: "Sea" or "the great green," is an androgynous, fecundity deity, associated with the Mediterranean Sea.